Going On Holiday

Mary Auld

W
FRANKLIN WATTS
LONDON • SYDNEY

Everyone likes to go away on holiday. It's a time to relax and have fun with your family.

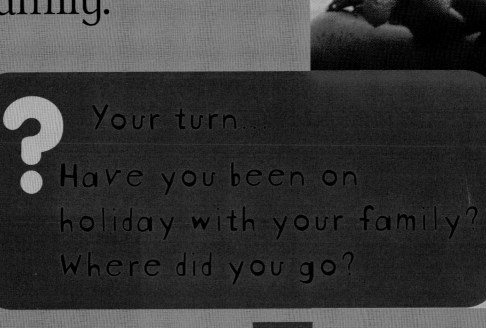

? Your turn...

Have you been on holiday with your family? Where did you go?

Sarah and her granny choose where to go on holiday together.

Sarah says:

"Gran and I like the same sort of holidays – somewhere hot and sunny."

When it is time to go
away, Lynne and her twin,
Becky, help to pack.

People travel in different ways to go on holiday. Sometimes we go by car.

Sometimes we go by train or coach. Meera holds Mum's hand tightly at the station.

? Your turn...

What way do you like to travel on holiday?

Sometimes we go away on holiday in an aeroplane. First we have to go to the airport.

Kurt says:
"I raced Dad and my brother to the check-in counter."

8

Then we get on the plane and fly to another airport, often in another country.

Fleur says:
"It's exciting arriving in a new country – even if it's raining!"

Sometimes we visit relatives for a holiday. Duncan loves staying with his grandparents.

? Your turn...

Which relatives do you go to stay with? What do you like doing there?

We can go on holiday just about anywhere. We can visit a big city ...

... or go walking in the country.

Of course, the best holidays are by the sea!

Your turn...

Why do you think so many families go on holiday by the sea?

When we're away, we need
somewhere to stay. A tent
makes a cosy holiday home.

So does a caravan.

❝ Gwen says:
"I love our caravan — it's like taking your home on holiday with you."

Sometimes people stay at a hotel or rent an apartment for the family.

? Your turn...

What sort of place would you like to stay in on holiday?

Harry's family found an apartment in a block with its own swimming pool.

On holiday, we take photos
and buy souvenirs.

Back home, we can look at them and remember our trip.

66 Hailey says:

"Granny and I laugh all over again when we look at the photos of us playing in the waves."

Where would you like to go on holiday with your family?

Some things to do

With your friends, make a collection of photos of your family holidays. Tell each other about where you went and what you did.

Plan 'the best holiday ever'. Where would you go? What would you do? Make a list of what you would need to pack.

Ask your grandparents or parents to tell you about holidays they went on as children. How were they different from today?

Sometimes we just have holidays at home. Write a story or poem about a holiday where you didn't go anywhere.

About this book

The aim of this book is to give children the opportunity to explore what their family means to them and their role within it in a positive and celebratory way. In particular it emphasises the importance of care and support within the family. It also encourages children to compare their own experiences with other people, recognising similarities and differences and respecting these as part of daily life.

Children will get pleasure out of looking at this book on their own. However, sharing the book on a one-to-one basis or within a group will also be very rewarding. Just talking about the main text and pictures is a good starting point, while the panels also prompt discussion:
• Question panels ask children to talk directly about their own experiences and feelings.
• Quote panels encourage them to think further by comparing their experiences with those of other children.

First published in 2007 by
Franklin Watts, 338 Euston Road
London NW1 3BH

Franklin Watts Australia
Level 17/207 Kent Street
Sydney NSW 2000

Copyright © Franklin Watts 2007
A CIP catalogue record for this book is available from the British Library.
Dewey classification: 790.1

ISBN: 978 0 7496 7625 4

Series editor: Rachel Cooke
Art director: Jonathan Hair
Design: Jason Anscomb

Picture credits: AM Corporation/Alamy: 16. James De Bounevialle/Photofusion: 13. Kevin Dodge/Corbis: 11. Stan Gamester/Photofusion: 19. Grace/zefa/Corbis: cover, 8. S & R Greenhill: 7, 9, 12, 14. LWA-Dann Tardiff/Corbis: 18. David Montford/Photofusion: 22. Picture Partners/Alamy: 5, 6, 21. Ariel Skelley/Corbis: 3. Paul Thompson/Corbis: 20. Libby Welch/Photofusion: 4. Frances Western/Photofusion: 17. Every attempt has been made to clear copyright. Should there be any inadvertent omission please apply to the publisher for rectification.

Please note that some of the pictures in this book have been posed by models.

Printed in China

Franklin Watts is a division of Hachette Children's Books, an Hachette Livre UK company.